The Sweet, The Sour, And Everything in Between

Natalie Marie

The Sweet, The Sour, And Everything in Between

Natalie Marie

ISBN: 9798597588940

Cover Art by Islam Farid
@islamsfarid
Illustrations by Peppermint Lines
@peppermintlines

To my readers,

Never allow anyone
to rob you of your sweetness.
Never give up
on finding love and happiness.
Never stop learning and growing.

You deserve the love and life you desire.

CONTENTS

<u>Preface</u>

I've always kept these words in between
the pages of my notebook, or tucked away in
an app in my phone. Writing has always been a
safety outlet for my emotions, a way to heal
from and deal with the ups and downs of life,
and a way to organize my thoughts and
process my feelings.

This book is a compilation of poetry I
wrote back when I was a teenager (revised and
edited), as well as poems I've written over the
past couple of years, to now. Some poems are
also inspired by the events that take place
around me. I share with you my experiences of
falling in love with people who, in the end,
were careless with my heart and made me feel
foolish for wearing my heart on my sleeve.

As I've gotten older, I've come to
realize that holding onto anger, regrets and the
past does *nothing* but make you miserable. We
cannot change what has already been done. I
thought about how, whenever I felt sad or
lonely, reading poetry always made me feel less
alone. It has especially played a big part in my
healing from relationships.

I thought what if maybe I could do that
for others, too? What if my words could give

at least *one* person the courage to walk away from a toxic relationship, or push them to put themselves first?

So here it is: My first poetry book. I hope you find something that resonates with you.

<u>Epigraph</u>

I remember my first real heartbreak:

I was so angry. Not just towards myself for ignoring the red flags, but also towards:

Relationships.
Love.
Men.

I remember telling myself I *never* wanted to feel that way again:

Vulnerable.
Stupid.
Heartbroken.

So miserable that I couldn't even get out of bed. Headaches (and eye-aches) from crying myself to sleep.

I remember thinking this is where I start to put myself first:

I went to College. Received a Diploma.
Got a full time job in the field I studied in.
I did the best I could to work on *me*.

**But during that time, I shut men out
completely:**

I became bitter.
I didn't date — I had no desire to.
I don't even think I did this on purpose; it was
almost like a defence mechanism.

**I remember, this is where the feeling of
regret began to surface, and I realized…**

You can miss out on so much by

holding onto the past,
refusing to let yourself live
        and love

        all because of one bad experience.

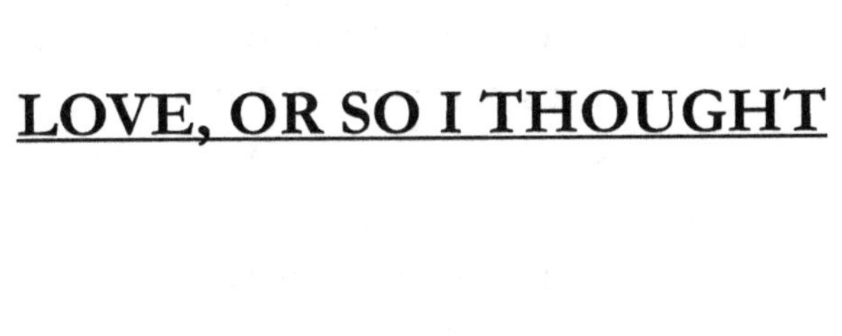

LOVE, OR SO I THOUGHT

You said you wanted to be with me,
but it's not the right time.

I should've known right then,
that you'd never fully be mine.

I knew I was falling for you
when your smile
lit up my entire world,
like the Northern lights
glistening in the night sky.

I knew I was falling for you
between late night conversations,
under the stars and the moon.
I stayed up till daybreak
just to keep talking to you.

I knew I was falling for you
when we'd laugh until our bellies ached,
eating snacks and staying up late.

I knew I was falling for you
when I adored the way
my name sounded coming
from your mouth,
your voice as deep as the ocean
and as smooth as silk.
Softly laid kisses
placed on my neck,
warm little snuggles,
cuddled up in bed.

Watching our favourite movies
and singing our favourite songs,
looking at you and knowing
I was right all along.

That's when I knew…

I had

f
 a
  l
   l
    e
     n

for you.

You sent flowers to my work
with a little note that read:

From your not-so-secret admirer

I didn't expect that gesture,
so it meant so much more to me

than the actual flowers.

—the smallest acts have the greatest impact

You awakened all five of my senses:

When I first saw you,
I was drawn to your energy.
Captivated by your brown eyes,
how they twinkled under the dim light,
like stars in a sapphire sky.

When I held you,
taking in your cologne,
the smell of bergamot
and sandalwood lingered
on my skin.
It took me to a place,
I had never been.

When you touched me,
the hairs on my arm rose,
sending a shiver down my spine.
Oh how that feeling,
felt so divine.

The dulcet tones of your voice,
the silly things you'd say,
the sweet words you'd speak to me
empowered me every day.

Our drunk laughter, the highest of highs.
The taste of your lips
after a glass or two of wine,
    had me feeling grateful
        that you were mine.

"Come over?"

—the text I couldn't wait to receive

The last night we spent together,
we walked around outside in the cold,
dark winter.
Told our friends we'd be
back for the countdown,
but got so caught up in each other,
just fooling around.
We suffered in the cold just to
be alone a while longer,
as we laughed, our teeth chattered.

I hoped this night
wouldn't end too soon,
I remember your voice, your laugh,
and your shaking hands, too.
The way you were so unsure,
the way you'd take out your phone
to check the time, then put your
hand in my pocket and held mine.

You'd tell me you miss me
almost every night since then.
And I remember when you'd text me
almost every day and when,
we'd send each other long paragraphs
about how we felt about each other.

I remember when I read your words,
how the butterflies began to flutter.

And at the stroke of twelve,
your lips met mine.
We never made it back
by midnight.

—*New Years Eve*

I love it
when you tell me
how you feel
whether that entails
how much you *love me,*
or how much
you *want me.*

—*communication turns me on*

My mind drifts back
to that weekend in Niagara Falls.
Where we went wine tasting,
played mini golf, and went on nightly strolls.

Empty streets, streetlights,
the sound of crickets in the night,
and the odd one or two cars passing by.
Stopping at shops to buy a souvenir:
*A magnet, a keychain,
a mug with the year.*

I am filled with warmth
thinking back to Jamaica;
our first trip together.
Climbing Dunn's River Falls,
Bob Marley's Nine Mile tour.
We enjoyed the beach,
the live shows,
and soaked up the sun,
knowing back home,
it was gloomy and cold.

The Luminous Lagoon —
Where I had to hold onto you,
because I don't know how to swim,

but still wanted to experience
the magical glow that surrounded
us as we jumped in.

And how could I forget Montreal?

It is where you first told me
you loved me,
          after all.

—*our adventures*

I like my space,

But I also like filling it with you.

"It was always you,"

you whispered.

"It still is."

You always had a way with words,
and I always felt them deep within my soul.
But it's words like that
that can either crush you to pieces,
or make you eminently whole.

Uncertainty fills my mind,
flooding my thoughts.
Doubts float by in
a pool of emotions.
Lack of communication
on both our parts,
I wait for you to
recite the words I long to hear.
Maybe it was too soon to say,
maybe I could've said something too,
but I hold back, in fear of looking too
clingy, or
                p u s h i n g   y o u   a w a y.

A tide rolls in,
I let it run its course.
I withdraw my questions
and allow them to drown
in a sea of controversial actions:

Like when you'd leave me in the deep end,
so you could play beer pong on the shore.

Or when we'd have a conversation,
and you'd decide it wasn't worth having
anymore.

I grab onto the life preserver,
I've swallowed too much water…

How could I allow myself to wrestle
with my own introspection,
when all I had to do
was ask you your intentions?

One day I feel special,
and showered with your love.

        The next I don't hear from you,
        not even a text to say what's up.

It's not like I expect you
to always make the first move

        but sometimes I test you,
        when I always do.

I'm more familiar with
what-ifs and could've-beens,
misery and disappointment,
misunderstandings and miscommunications,
infatuation and lust.

—please forgive me for expecting the worst

Do you ever think back to
the nights we shared together?
When passion would stem
from every corner of your bed,
your sheets drenched in the nectar
that sits between my thighs.
Satisfied sighs fill your room,
but they only last for a second.
I ask,

do you regret anything or
wish you had loved me better?

As honeyed words spill from your lips,
I roll over and you'd think I'd feel lighter,
But instead,

I'm heavier than ever.

I stare at the pile of clothes
that lay upon the floor, and wonder:

Will you still wear any of the clothes
I bought you when I'm gone?

Will you think of me when
you put them on?

Sugar-coated lies
escape your lips once more,
and still, I don't feel any better…

*I'm still **heavier** than ever.*

What is it about me
that's so easy to ignore?
Is it because you know I'll be here,
when you come knocking at my door?

What is it about me
that makes it so easy to walk away?
What is it about you
that makes me desperately want you to stay?

I've been craving the sand
between my toes,
the ocean waves
crashing over my feet.
Maybe I'm selfish

for wanting you to stay
as we write our names
in the sand

watching…

                as it gets washed

                                away.

—just like our love

The saddest part
about relationships that end,
is that you build
a friendship with that person.
You share so much of yourself with them,
then one day,
something happens:

They betray you.

> *You betray them.*

Things don't work out.

> *You realize you're going
> down different paths…*

If you're lucky,
you can remain good friends.

But I think we both know

> that's not how it usually ends.

"Sorry," you say.
But somehow it doesn't feel genuine.

Your shifting eyes and crocodile tears,
the sensation of your timid embrace.
The hesitation in your voice,
the shame painted on your face.

I feel sick to my stomach
as I give you the benefit of the doubt.

For if you were truly sorry,
you would've felt the guilt
long before I found out.

—unfaithful

Your eyes,
they wander.
Your soul,
restless and unsatisfied.
Your heart,
eager and hungry.
I always thought I wasn't doing enough,
but it turns out,
you were just greedy.

I think you're a good person
with good intentions.
But sadly,

the results of your intentions
don't turn out so good.

Like getting burned in a fire,

there's an adrenaline rush,
the thrill of impending danger.
Then suddenly, the flames get
bigger
        and
                bigger, setting you ablaze.

You scream, squall, ache,
consequently,
        there will be scars.

The scars will eventually heal,
but the memories
will never completely go
away.

—*love*

I would be lying if I said
I didn't see the signs.
The alarms kept going off,
but I snoozed them every time.
I made excuses for you
because I wanted to believe
that the signs were wrong,
and the alarms were faulty.

I want to cross you

out,

like

blackout

poetry

leaving the

good

parts.

I get caught
between
wanting you back
and wanting to tell you
to go fuck yourself.

I get caught
between
forgiving you
and hating your guts.

I get caught
between
wanting to kiss and hold you,
and never wanting to
touch or see you again.

—the sweet, the sour & everything in between

I've noticed I don't write
when I'm happy.
I don't even really write
when I'm in love.
Only when my heart is broken
do the words pour
           out
               of
                  me.

The ink in my pen
has exploded all over
my hands — it's a sign…

*to wash them clean
of you and me.*

It was love,
or so I thought.

Perhaps we were
too young
      too immature
            too impulsive
to really know what love was.

THE (BITTER) HEARTACHE

There you go again,
emotionally investing
yourself into others
as if you haven't
been burned before.

There you go again,
believing everybody
will love you
the same way that
you love them.

  —I hate it when I do that

We were like two magnets:

No matter how hard we tried
to stay apart,
we just kept being pulled
towards each other,

but never meant to touch.

The days go by
so quickly,
and things just haven't been
how they used to be.
I pictured my summer
so differently,
I pictured
you and me.

But just like the seasons,
feelings change,
people change,
they come
and they go.
And I am left
with memories
filled of
someone
I used
to know.

—*changes*

You say you miss me,
you say you love me,
but I think you're just in love
with the *idea* of me,
this image of me
you've embedded
into your head.

Your arms embrace me like a summer's day,
wrapping your warmth around my body.
You colour my soul with the leaves of fall,
spoil me with the flowers of spring,
watch me grow as the rain nourishes me,
then leave me
              with the coldness
of winter.

Tried to keep myself from falling,
but it happened so quick.
Used to look forward
to talking to you,
                 seeing you,
now it makes me sick.

I knew what I should've done,
              should've said,
but didn't know it wouldn't last.
I think back to everything
you've said to me,
though I know it's in the past.

Were they lies, or did you mean it?

Your magnetic charm made me
oblivious to it all.
I didn't even stop to think that
you may miss me
         when I
            f
              a
            l
              l.

Now I hate that I left myself vulnerable.
Opened my heart to you
and watched it all
                    crumble.
I let it get the best of me,
wore my heart on my damn sleeve.
Didn't think you'd lie and hurt me,
didn't think you'd leave.

I always told myself I'd never rush things,
but clearly I don't listen.
Spoke my mind, said how I felt,
but don't seem to learn my lesson.

All I know is I don't want to let you go,
because when I said
I don't want to lose you,
I meant it more than you know.

You never took me seriously,
you always saw me as a joke.
I guess that's why you played me
so gracefully
with the words that you spoke.

Distract me with your touch,
so I wouldn't suspect your
deceitful tongue.
Keeping me on the sidelines,
while I believed I was the only one.

But I'm glad I could be your
amusement for a while,
someone to toy with until
you found someone else.

I used to think I was to blame
for everything that went wrong,
but I've finally realized
that it was you all along.

You couldn't see that what
you did was completely unfair;
I shouldn't be feeling like this,
I shouldn't even care.

I can't fight this fight anymore,
and I'm tired of being the only one
who tries.

*I fought for the truth
in a sea full of lies.*

Once upon a time,
we could've been something special.
We could've been good for each other,
but we took different paths,
lived different lives,
and chose different people
with whom to spend our time.

See,
you and me,
we were a fantasy.
I fantasized about you,
about us,
about you and her.
I fantasized about you,
touching me,
touching her.
I almost lost sight
of reality.

When it finally set in,
I accepted the fact
that we would never be,
and I no longer wanted to live
in a fantasy.

You only wanted me when
it was most convenient
for you…

I was just an afterthought,
*   after you finished fucking her.*

You even said,
*"It's all fun and games
until someone gets hurt (you)."*

You joked but,
little did I know
it would turn out to be true.

*—there's a little truth behind every
"I'm just kidding"*

It must be nice to tell
every girl the same thing,
make every girl feel like she's
special and beautiful
and that to you, *she means something.*
It must be nice to make her think
you're into her, hold her hand
and tell her what she wants to hear.

And I'm more than a fool
to fall for your shit
more than once in one year.

I don't know what you want from me,
I don't understand
what goes through your mind
when you start to hold my hand.
To think you may actually feel something
for me — how stupid could I get?
I guess it's only natural to say

sometimes I wish we never met.

    —rebound

You think you're so damn perfect,
sorry to say, but you're actually far from it.
You know what's right,
but you choose to do the opposite.

Your ego clouds your vision,
your every decision.
Your ears are open,
but you never listen.
You fail to see your faults,
your mistakes, your flaws,
you fail to see you were wrong,
because you only see what you want.

—*blinded by your ego*

Your actions speak louder than your words.
Much louder.

All you had to do
was say you're not interested,
rejection sucks, but I'm a big girl,
I can take it.

Your silence tells me all the things
you weren't man enough to say.
I handed out so many chances
            and you threw them *all* away.

—*ghosted*

I don't like that sneaky shit.
That *being-kept-in-the-dark* type shit.

I don't do well with secret conversations
The ones r
      e
     t
    r
   a
  c
 t
 e
d

when the day is done.

I am not your mistress, so quit treating me like one.

Hide me away.
Stash me underneath your bed.
Then pull me out
when you're ready to play.

Like an old toy you're ashamed of,
and only take out when she's not around.

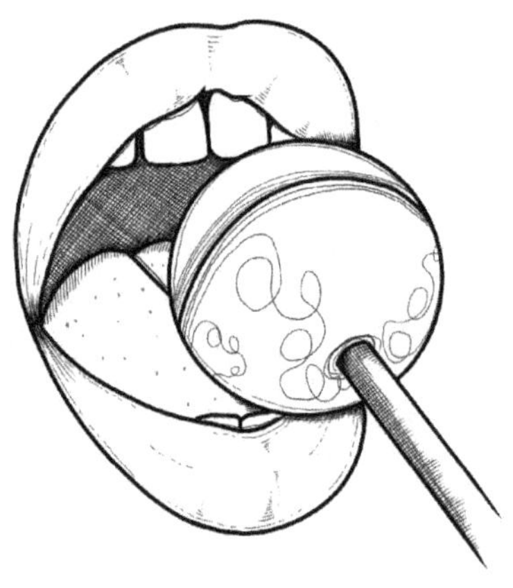

I devoured your words
and the sweetness of your lies
gave me cavities.

I should've loved you in moderation.

The problem is
I give too much of my heart
to people who only give me
a fraction of theirs.

They don't break my heart,

I break my own.

You have no idea
The lengths I had to go
To refrain from breaking
Every rule
Every moral
Every belief
I had instilled inside of me.

—and I still broke them to some extent

There is nothing worse
than having a gut feeling
about something and
ignoring it
believing you are just over-thinking
only for it to turn out
to be right
all along.

—know when to trust your gut

I was afraid of being alone,
not realizing that staying with you
was the

loneliest

place to be.

You think I'm clueless
because I don't call you out
on the things I notice every day.
But these eyes observe more
than what this mouth will say.

If you were finding yourself attracted
to somebody else,
the best thing you could've done
was be honest,

not only with me,

                    but with yourself.

*—if you're going to hurt me,
hurt me with the truth*

Don't feel bad for him.

Yes, you had good times —
it was bittersweet.

But do you remember when
he was lying through his teeth?

Remember all the times
you felt alone while in his presence?
When his phone would be
glued to his hand,
but would take hours to
respond to your message?
Don't second guess yourself,
don't be afraid to lose him,
              as a lover or a friend…

Remember,

while you were being faithful to him,
and only wanting his attention,
he was giving his to
              another woman.

You were with her
the entire time you were with me.
Posting pictures of you
painting her toes,
looking all sweet.

You really had the nerve
to tell me you were 'just friends'
and that you weren't with her again.
I find it funny that
you still couldn't tell me the truth
even after I messaged her
and had written proof.

Witty one-liners
on every single picture.
Matched with her captions,
you thought I'd never find her.

You didn't even try to hide it:
left it there for all to see,
as if you had no worry
if it was potentially seen by me.

And I just want to let you know,
that you're a shitty fucking cheat.

When I feel I don't get
the same love I give in return,
I pull back.

A fool I once was,
a fool I'll *never* be again.

All I know
is that
I don't
want to be
the one
you run to
when things
don't work out
with her.

—rebound II

You walk past me like I'm not even there.
You think I don't notice,
but I know you don't care.
I feel invisible, like the air I breathe.
I feel as meaningless, as the words I speak.

I put on an act, pretend to be happy,
trick myself and everybody else around me.
Artificial smiles spread across my face,
to mask the sting I feel every day.
I am fighting for something
that doesn't want to be fought for,
it's frustrating — *so frustrating* —
but I think it's time I close this door.

—when they don't give you closure,
you must give it to yourself

I'm sorry
if I'm ever not
what you need
at times
when you need it most.

Like a kick to the throat,
and a punch to the chest.
A knife in the back,
and a head full of stress.
It sounds like a whisper,
but slowly turns to a scream.
A bunch of little voices,
destroy my self-esteem.
It feels like my ribcage
has been torn and distressed.
My appetite has cut and

                       I'm feeling

depressed.

—heartache

You broke me
into a million tiny pieces
shattered across the floor.
And although I picked myself up
and put the pieces back together,
I continued to move forward cautiously,
afraid to

b
 r
  e
   a
    k
        again.

  —*fragile*

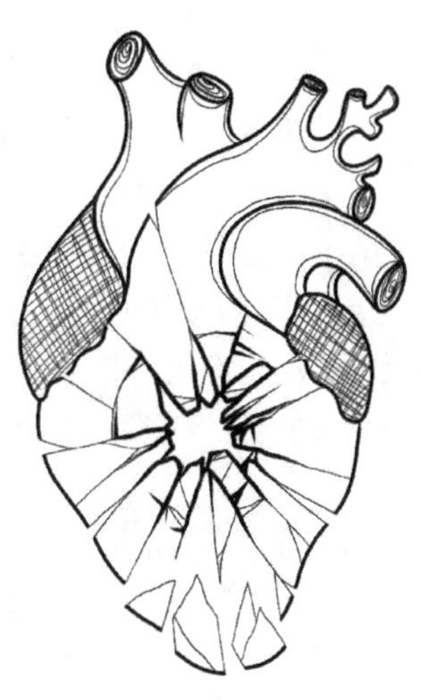

Flirting and hitting on someone else
while in a relationship is *cheating*.
Being emotionally invested in someone else
while in a relationship is *cheating*.

My definition, as you can see,
goes beyond white linen sheets.
One click, one swipe, one text, one call…
that device in your hand will do it all.

You made yourself available,
and you opened the door
for possibly more
and if given the chance,
I have no doubt that you would've taken it.

There is nothing friendly or innocent
about a man or a woman
telling someone who is **not their partner**
how fine and sexy they are,
and how their hotness is
"overheating your phone."

Infidelity has become so easy,
you don't even have to leave your home.

I could be the warmest person
or the coldest person you've ever met.
The temperature depends
on how you treat me.

Sometimes
when you feel too much
you start to wish you'd feel nothing at all.

So I turned off my emotions
as a way of protecting myself.

I left because I realized that
my happiness,
my mental and emotional health,
and my peace of mind
were more important than staying
with someone who was careless
with my feelings and
disrespectful to our relationship.

    —I loved you, but I love me more

Don't be fooled
into thinking
that I cannot be alone
simply because
I enjoy your company
and want you around me.

—as an introvert, I also enjoy my own presence

I'm sorry for wasting your time.
But I have to say,

I'm more sorry for wasting mine.

I didn't like the bitter taste in my mouth
every time I drank from
the fountain of love.
I consumed words that sounded beautiful,
paired with actions that were ugly.
"I love you's" thrown around
like a game of catch.
Be better, not bitter
is what I tell myself.

I don't want to lose my sweet.

MISSED OPPORTUNITIES

I wish
I could travel back in time
and live my life differently.
There are so many things I'd do over,
so many opportunities I would take.
I would give more chances, take more risks,
and not be so afraid to try new things.

I try not to live with regrets,
but I feel like every chance
that I didn't take finds its way back to me,
leaving me with the burning question:

Am I really living?

Such silly things I allow to stress me out
and fatigue my brain.
And even though I know better,
I can't help but feel
like I'm just living day-by-day…
            Letting people
                        and opportunities
            pass me by.

—*missed opportunities*

I distance myself from people,
and then wonder why
they are so distant.

I choose to walk alone,
and then wonder why
there is nobody by my side.

I don't want to be
the centre of attention,
yet I want to be heard and seen.

I push people away,
and then question
why nobody wants to stay.

—*a walking paradox*

Guarded and lonely —
I don't know how to

                                              escape

these walls I helped build.

Isn't it sad…

how our first reaction to emotions
is to hide or fight them?

I will admit that I have done this —
we all have at some point —
and I've learned that it only
makes us miss opportunities,
and we hurt ourselves
when regret creeps in.

—missed opportunities II

It's 1:15 a.m.

I sit here,
grieving those
who've done me wrong,
while they let go
                and move on.
New partners, new lives,
allow new emotions to reside
inside of them.

Reminiscing about my youth,
all the adventures I went on,
and all the ones I missed out on.
The memories feel so close,
yet so far away.
I feel like I could almost touch them.

But when I reach out my hand,

                they dissipate.

I've touched the forbidden fruit —
I nibbled at it once or twice,
but I never took a bite.
I knew that if I did,
my subconscious would
haunt me at night.

But I get so angry,
that sometimes
there are days
when I wish
I just ate
the *whole*
damn
fruit.

  —sometimes I get tired of being the 'good' girl

I wanted not to care.

I wanted not to think so much about the "right" decisions and the consequences. I wanted to, for once, live on the edge, make dumb decisions and regret the things that I've done, rather than the things that I didn't. I wanted not to be phased by anything a man did to me. I wanted to be heartless,

so that I could hurt less.

One minute you're sixteen,
young and innocent.
Full of life.
Full of hope.
Full of promise.

Then before you know it,
you're twenty-nine,
grown and knowledgeable.
Searching for your purpose in life.
Feeling hopeless, while remaining hopeful.

Desperately trying
to fulfill
every promise
you've made
to yourself.

The older I got,
the angrier I felt.

The angrier I felt,
the sadder I became.

The sadder I became,
the more hesitant I ended up being.

The more hesitant I ended up being,
the less I allowed myself to experience.

I'm starting to feel
awkward and uncomfortable
when family or friends
ask me if I'm seeing anybody.

I'm starting to feel
like I will never find someone
I can build something
meaningful with.

I'm starting to feel more

disconnected

than connected

with *love,*

with *people,*

with *myself.*

I beat myself up
for staying alone as long as I did.
I wish someone would've been there
to tell me,
to encourage me,
to reassure me
that it was okay
to hurt again.
to feel again.

But I think it was the fear
of that heartbroken feeling
that made me reluctant to
become vulnerable again,
rather than
the fear
to *love*
itself.

But why do I weep,
over the things I should be proud
I didn't do?

It feels like these days
I've been isolated,
stuck in the same spot
I've been in for weeks.
My feet feel heavy,
my stomach is in knots…

Why do we give so much power
to such negative thoughts?

I never understood the concept
of using people.
I don't know *how*
to use people.
I don't know how
to sink my teeth
into their delicate heart
for my own sick pleasure

        with no intention
            to stick around.

I decided to finally push myself
to go on a couple dates.
I decided not to force it,
I left it up to fate.

I met one guy,
but he didn't give me butterflies.
I tried to give him a chance,
but he didn't make my heart dance.

I just couldn't see him
as more than a friend.
I wanted to but,
it's not in my nature to pretend.

It wasn't his fault,
but I began to wonder
if all those years I spent
avoiding romance
made connecting
            even harder.

I didn't realize how heavy
my regrets were
until I started to say
them out loud.

To cling to them for
years seems like
such a waste of time,
a waste of energy.

As they released
from my every breath,

I slowly felt the weight of each of them

lift
    off
        my chest.

I like to think of moments
like a shooting star:
beautiful,
but fleeting.

Try not to miss them.

Appreciate life,
and how lucky we are to
experience it.

Don't get so caught up
in the things you didn't do
that you forget to do the things
you still have the chance to.

THE HEALING

My love is like honey,
delicate and sweet.
I watch it overflow,
dripping at your feet.

Slowly but surely,
it becomes too much.
Like the wings of a butterfly,
tender to the touch.

As a pool of honey surrounds you,
you try desperately to break free.
If this is love, then darling
I'll pour the rest into me.

—*love yourself first*

The emptiness
I used to feel
when I didn't
see your name
pop up on my phone
is slowly
      fading
           away.

Think of your relationship with them
as an experience,
not time wasted.

—*my response to pg. 89*

Dear Self,

You are worthy of love.
Devoted, kind, fun, passionate love.
You are worthy of happiness.
You are worthy of success.
You are worthy of being committed to.

Not everyone has the same intentions,
not everyone wants to hurt you.
Not everyone thinks you're not good
enough.
You **ARE** good enough —
For yourself, your family, your friends,
and for someone who can and will truly
appreciate your value and
who you are as a person.

Let go of the past.
Let go of what has hurt you,
and bruised your mind, your heart, your
soul.

Start fresh.
Make peace with the past, the ache,
the experiences — *positive and negative.*

Do not bring them up to compare
in arguments or out of anger.
Don't grant your insecurities permission
to ruin something great.

Focus on the present.
Train your mind to be consistent this way.
Do not allow yourself to be brought back
down the path of comparing
the old to the new.
Look ahead. Look forward.

Step outside your comfort zone.
Choose a goal and stick to it.
Consistency is key to change and improvement.

When things are going well,
it doesn't mean that it's "too good to be
true."
Have faith that there are people out there
who want the best for you.

Embrace the good.
It doesn't always mean
it will follow with something bad.
Be kind.
Be honest.
Be trusting.

You have dealt with many "fuck boys"
who have made you doubt
the men who are not.

In case you forget, remember these words:

I. Am. Worthy.

It's not all my fault,
I shouldn't take all the blame.
I hope you understand
where I was coming from,
even if you didn't understand
the pain.

I am constantly
trying to improve
and become a better
version of myself.

I am constantly
looking for ways
to be happy with
the person I was,
                  the person I am,
and the person I will become.

Trying to find peace
where there is only chaos
but I'll find balance.

—*peace vs chaos*

I have a lot that I need to work on
when it comes to myself.
I've realized every long-term or short-term
relationship I've had was not all *their* fault,
but also *mine.*
I may have, in some way, played a toxic role,
not realizing it at the time.

　　—own your shit

I ripped up and deleted
almost all our photos together.
A part of me wishes I hadn't,
             not because I miss you,
but because they were still memories.
You were a part of my life,
and although we didn't last,
it was still proof that there was an *us*.

I experienced more with you
in the one year we were together
than I experienced with anyone, ever.

It was raw.
It was passionate.
It was adventurous.
It was beautiful.

—I don't regret you

You made me feel so *alive*
after feeling *nothing*
for the longest time.

Thank you for reminding me
what it felt like
to open my heart again.

I want to get caught up
in his mess,
and tangled up
in his love.

I want to
            o p e n up,
reveal my secrets to someone.
Things I've never shared before,
the things I've always felt uncomfortable to.

No regrets,
no discomfort,
just honest conversation,
            and no complication.

　　—a passionate thought

I am working
on not letting
the words, actions and energy
of other people
affect me.

Do what you feel is right in the moment.

Take chances,
even if they seem scary at first.
Try not to think too much
or too hard about things.
Be more spontaneous.
Be more open-minded.
Go on more adventures.
Travel.
Do what makes YOU happy.
Live your best life.

After all,
we've only got one.

—a list of things to do moving forward

I am a work in progress.

But I will progress.

The more I love
the *parts* of myself
I used to want to change,
the more I love myself *completely.*

It is so liberating:

The feeling after letting go of someone
you never thought you could let go of.

Finally breaking free of the chains
that you've been bound to for so long.

Finally standing up for yourself
and being loud and clear
about what you want.

The feeling of freedom
coursing
through
your veins.

Every decision I've ever made
has led me to this very moment.
Sure, there are days I wish I could
go back and change certain things,
but that could've led to a totally different
life.

—and I wouldn't switch this life for anything

I awake to the sound of the rain
pinging against the glass
of my bedroom window.

At first, I feel sad about
the way things ended with you.

My blinds are closed,
but I can see that it's overcast
through the small open space.
I rub my eyes,
and try to muster up the energy
to get out of bed and start the day.

But instead, I lay here,
I turn my attention back
to the sound of the rain,

Tap tap tap.

I breathe a deep sigh of relief.

And for a moment,
I feel peace.

I write because it helps me
to cope with what I feel.
I write because it's the only thing
that helps me to heal.
I write in hopes that maybe somebody
out there can relate to what I write,
and we both can find some comfort
knowing we are not alone tonight.

—why I write

The moon is illuminated
in the dark, star-lit sky
The sun is not the only one
with the desire to shine.

—even in the darkness,
we can shine our light on the world

I dried my tears,
fixed my make-up,
inhaled deeply, then exhaled.
Told myself everything happens
for a reason, and not to get deterred.

I feed myself positive affirmations,
instead of poisoning myself
with negative words.

—the way you speak to yourself is important

When I sit and reflect,
I no longer wish to be any way
but the way that I am.
I will no longer allow missed
opportunities to haunt me.
Because maybe,
                    just maybe,

those opportunities
        were missed
                for a reason.

—*missed opportunities III*

I bought myself flowers
and wrote myself a love letter.
I told myself I was beautiful
and encouraged myself to do better.
I tattooed *"love yourself first"* on my forearm
as a reminder to do just that.

I think we all need
to remember
that the only opinion
about ourselves
that should really matter
is our own.

Morning.
Golden sunlight
Piercing through my window
A new day, fresh new beginnings…
I rise.

Plant seeds into your wounds,
and cover them with the Earth's soil.
Cry if you must — the tears
will help you grow from this.
Just as we appreciate the beauty
after nature's gloom,
the world will see the beauty
of your petals when they bloom.

—the healing

REKINDLED LOVE

And just like that,
you came back into my life
as if you never even left.

An old flame

that never

went dull.

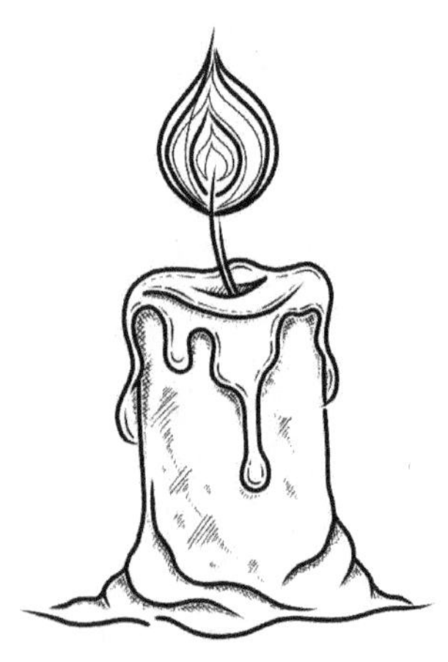

143

Twelve years rolled past,
and we never looked back.
I never imagined that
we'd reconnect, and if we did,
we'd just be friendly acquaintances.
Going back to someone I've dated before
is not something that I do.
But *you*…

You are the exception.

I knew you were something special
when I would act
like a total jerk to you
in my most insecure or vulnerable moments,

and you **still** *wanted to be with me.*

I want to see myself through your eyes,
I want to know what it's like
to step outside my body,
and meet myself for the first time…

Would I like her?

Would I still think of her the same,

or would my perception of her change?

Would it be like every other day,
staring at my own reflection?

Maybe my voice would have
a different intonation.

Would I still be self-conscious of my narration?

Your eyes have seen me at my best,
but also at my worst:

hair in tangles,
eyebrows unkempt,
no make-up on,
feeling restless.

You see beauty where I see flaw.
How I'd love to catch a glimpse
of what it is about me
that seems to leave you

in awe.

When we're together,
all the hours in the day
are never enough for me.
And when we're apart,
it feels like eternity.

I look at you
and all I can think
is how grateful I am
that we found our way
back to each other.

Home —
We call it a person
We call it a place
We call it a feeling
We can never replace.
"Home is where the heart is,"
I'm sure you know the saying.

As long as I feel home with you,
it is where I'm staying.

I fell in love with the sky
the way I fell in love with you.
Admiring the colours it creates,
just like I admire you.
Cotton candy clouds,
bursting with purple, pink,
yellow and orange hues.
As we watched the sunrise
and the sunset together,
I realized I wanted to start
    and end
        each day with you.

It is not in our similarities,

but in our *differences*

that we try to understand each other.

Morning coffee /Afternoon walks /
Evening bike rides / Our daily talks /
Movie nights and cuddles / Video games /
Taking photos / Our date nights / Shooting
and editing videos / Reading together /
Writing poetry / Supporting and inspiring each
other

—a list of what makes me happy

Hold me in your arms
a little while longer,
let me nestle up into your neck.
You are my comfort;
with you, I feel safe.
I close my eyes, breathe you in
and get lost
in your embrace.

Share with me
your deepest desires;
the ones you carry in your heart,
but don't allow anyone to see.

Love me harder
on days
when it's
hard for me
to love myself.

The Sweet, The Sour & Everything in Between

I could feel the
sensation of longing
and adoration in your kiss.
Your lips taste like
freshly picked strawberries,
sweet, with hints of citrus,
just ripe enough to touch my lips.

I've always loved the way it felt
when it collided with mine.

—*euphoria*

You speak words
to me
that sound like
poetry.

There are places
you have touched me
that have nothing to do
with your hands.

You smell of sweet nostalgia,
taking me back to an innocent
                    and familiar time.

Life was so different then,
     we were just teenagers,
still trying to figure out our lives.

*You never were
             one for cologne.*
Overpowering notes of
basil and pepper,
     amber and cinnamon
was never your style.

You were simple.

*Natural.
             Fresh and clean —*
Irish Spring,
     with light notes
             of fabric softener
     in between.

          —my favourite scent

There is a calmness
in you
that seems to ease
the anxiety
in me.

Your calloused hands
have explored every inch of my body,
tracing every imperfection
like it was the most beautiful thing
you'd ever come across.

They have clung
onto the depths of my soul
with the patience and desire
to understand the
battered elements
of my being.

Who knew that something so rough
                    could be so soft?

Night falls
As I *fall* asleep in your arms.
Tender kisses placed upon my lips…
Amid the chaos, your light shines bright —-
Lovingly reminding me to be here, now.
I thank the stars for guiding you back to me
Each and every night.

I kept parts of myself
hidden away in the dark,
afraid of being seen,
to expose myself completely.

To my surprise,
you have shone the light
on the darkest parts of me.

I don't know what
the future holds
but I'll be there
when it unfolds.

Every sunrise
every storm
any weather
cold
or warm.

REMINDERS
TO YOU & ME

If you ever feel torn
between your heart and your head,
listen to your head —
Especially if your heart is leading you
back to what caused you heartache.

—head vs heart

It does more harm than good
to hold onto feelings and people
that no longer make you smile.

Do yourself a favour and release them.

Time spent in the dark
corners of your past
will not bring light
into your present.

I never said letting go was easy.

I never said you shouldn't give
a second chance.

But how many chances can one give,

until it is considered *too many?*

You can't fall in love
and think you'll come out unscathed.
That's the first wrong assumption
we all inevitably make.

You can't fall in love
and think you'll get along every night.
You're not always going to agree,
you're not always going to win the fight.

Love is not rainbows and sunshine,
it's thunderstorms
and rain showers in-between.
But you'll realize soon enough,
it's not about winning
when you're both on the same team.

There is always going to be
a moment in your life
when you sit back and reflect
on all the things you wish
you had done differently.

But you cannot dwell on it.

The past cannot be altered.

Never minimize
your feelings
to maximize
someone else's.

You are *not* to blame
for someone else's inability
to be faithful to you.

Don't allow him
to make you feel guilty
for being hurt by what *he* did.

Don't let him
make you feel like
it was *your* fault.

    —signs of a narcissist

Your growth is like a flower:

It needs
sunlight,
water,
patience,
and *love.*

But you can't rely on others
to give you those things anymore…

You must give it to yourself.

—*self-love*

The Sweet, The Sour & Everything in Between

Communicate how you feel.

Humans are not mind-readers.
I know we like to think they are,
or that they "should just know"
but when it comes down to it,
they don't know.

And they won't ever know,
unless you talk about it.
Share your emotions,
and how they made you feel,
if they made you feel a certain way.

If something is bothering you,
or if there's something
that you find difficult to express,
keep in mind that if you don't let it out,
you're only burdening yourself
and those emotions will manifest,
turning into something much bigger
than it needs to be.

—they will not see you,
if you keep hiding

You allowed yourself to get lost with him.
He drove you down this road
of self-deprecation.
He beat you down so badly
that you've forgotten
who you are, what you're worth
and what you deserve.

He was your friend.
Your lover.
Your confidant.
He betrayed you in the worst way.
I know it doesn't feel like it now,
but you will survive.

—I believe you will find yourself again

My words travel through one ear
and out the other, it seems…

You say you care too much,
and you always feel bad for him,
but,

don't you feel bad for you?

—I cannot help you,
if you're not willing to help yourself

I wish
you could see
how your actions
affect those around you.
I wish
you would take
a moment to self-reflect
and realize that drama
is not the answer
to a happy life.
I wish
you could see it
so clearly
that it pushes you
to become
a better version of yourself
in all that you do.
I wish you could see
that we are all *with* you,
not *against* you.

I can only hope that one day
you will find the strength to move on,
and the courage to love yourself
as much as you love the ones
who don't deserve it.

Your mind is a powerful thing:

You can either control it,
or let it control you.

You must forgive yourself
for all the mistakes you've made,
for all the hurtful things
people have said to you and
that you've said to yourself
that you now believe is true.
We have a tendency
to wallow in our emotions,
overthink them,
and punish ourselves.
Holding onto those negative feelings
and thoughts are poisonous,
and it will infect everyone around you.
Forgive yourself
          and love yourself.

You have the ability to evolve,
if you allow it.

You are running in

                 C
     S
                         I
     E

                     R
       L
          C

Expecting to end up
somewhere different
by never changing
where you are.

I think we judge ourselves too harshly.
I think we criticize our way of thinking,
how we do things and why we do them,
instead of just allowing ourselves to be who
we are. I think we feel like we are second-
rate, and we view others as more skilled, or
more desirable than we are. Comparing
ourselves to others is *automatic defeat*. We've
already decided that they are those things,
and we are not. While we endlessly give
compliments to others, we struggle to give
ourselves *one. We put ourselves through so much
unnecessary stress by doing this.* I want you to
put this book down and look at yourself in
the mirror, *really look at yourself,* and pick one
thing about yourself that you love. It could
be your eyes, your smile, your freckles, your
ability to empathize, *anything.* Write it down
and do this every day.

**We are not in competition with each
other.**

Embrace who you are.
Embrace it so much, you feel no shame.

And when you feel
change needs to happen,
                              let it.

For change means there is room for growth.

The next time you do your spring cleaning,
getting rid of clothes that don't fit you
and items you don't want,
don't forget to do the same with the people
who don't fit or deserve a place
in your life anymore.

    —declutter

When your best
doesn't seem
like it's good enough,
it's easy to feel
down and defeated,
but don't let that discourage you.

We once were infants
who couldn't even walk,
but what did we do?

We got up,
    and tried again.

    —baby steps

Sometimes
you have to do
what you *know*
is best for you,
instead of what
you *think* is
best for others.

Sometimes,
it is okay
to be selfish.

You have   so much
love inside of you. Don't pour
so much of it into one person.
Save some for yourself, so when
and if it's you they want to let
go of, you don't start
to resent your
capacity to
love.

THE SWEET, THE SOUR, AND EVERYTHING IN BETWEEN

The bitterness —
it comes and it goes.
Never fully releasing
its grip from my bones.

It comes when the love I put out
isn't reciprocated.
It comes when the care I show
isn't appreciated.
It comes when I feel like I'm
more invested than you.
It comes when I feel like
I give more of a fuck than you do.
It comes when I want to hold you,
and you want to leave.
I try not to give it
the attention it so often seeks.
The grip slowly loosens;
I don't feel so weak.

That's when I realized, without a doubt,

My fire
was never
for you
to put out.

Acknowledgements

Thank you to everyone who has supported me in my journey of writing this book. To my Mom and Dad, who have always had my back in everything I do. To my brother and my sister, for reading my poems and giving me unbiased feedback. To my boyfriend Tristan Jamaal, for his encouragement and support during the process of writing this book. To my cover artist Islam Farid, for bringing to life my vision for the cover of this book. To my illustrator Peppermint Lines, for creating the most breath-taking illustrations to accompany my poems. To my editor Kristian Porter, for ensuring that everything flowed seamlessly. And last, but definitely not least, to my friends and Instagram followers: For years, I have dreamt of compiling all my poems/thoughts into a book that can reach and hopefully help or inspire others. Without you, I probably never would've had the courage to do this at all. From the bottom of my heart, thank you.

Natalie Marie

Author Photo by @tristan.jamaal
Cover Art by @islamsfarid
Illustrations by @peppermintlines
Edited by @kristianportereditor

www.ingramcontent.com/pod-product-compliance
Lightning Source LLC
Chambersburg PA
CBHW071612150726
48000CB00004B/1685